17616

© Aladdin Books Ltd 1987

Designed and produced by
Aladdin Books Ltd
70 Old Compton Street
London W1

*First published in the
United States in 1987 by*
Franklin Watts
387 Park Avenue South
New York NY 10016

ISBN 0 531 10438 9

Library of Congress Catalog
Card Number: 87-50596

Printed in Belgium

Design   David West

Editor   Steve Parker

Researcher   Cecilia Weston-Baker

Illustrator   Peter Harper

The publishers wish to thank those
involved in producing this book,
especially Dr John Fry, doctor
of medicine and medical author.

613.8
S 837

Contents

UNDERSTANDING DRUGS

TOBACCO

Rob Stepney

FRANKLIN WATTS
New York · London · Toronto · Sydney

INTRODUCTION

Smoking tobacco is so common that it is almost impossible to see how odd it really is. The leaves of a plant are picked, dried, chopped up and rolled into paper tubes. We then stick the tubes into our mouths, light them and take the poison-laden smoke down into our lungs. Each time a person smokes a cigarette, it takes an average of five minutes off his or her life. This is about the same time it takes to smoke it.

Of all the drugs we have ever used, tobacco does by far the most damage. Heroin may cause hundreds of deaths each year. Smoking cigarettes causes hundreds of thousands of deaths. Each year smoking kills more than 300,000 people in the USA, around 50,000 people in Britain, and 16,000 in Australia.

At first, the harm done is difficult to grasp – because smoking is such a familiar, everyday thing. But so is death from the diseases that smoking causes. Think of how many people you have heard of dying from heart attacks or lung cancer.

For more than 30 years, we have known that smoking is a killer. Smokers know the dangers just as much as non-smokers. Most of us try smoking at some point in our lives. "Experimenting" like this is understandable. But many

Choose your poison: the number of cigarette brands is bewildering.

people continue to smoke. How can that be explained?

Most of the answer lies in nicotine, an addictive drug contained in tobacco smoke. Nicotine has many effects on the brain and body. The immediate effects are small, but over a period of a few months or years, they are enough to make you depend on the drug. You come to need smoking, almost like an alcoholic needs liquor.

Of course, you can give up. Millions of people have quit smoking. But the best thing by far is never to start. Not smoking is not being a killjoy. It's just a good way of not being killed. If you have started, the best thing is to stop. The sooner, the better.

This book explains what tobacco is, what it does, and why it may seem attractive. It also shows how to avoid the habit that takes away your freedom of choice – and could take away your life as well.

❛❛ Smoking is such an everyday thing. We must keep reminding ourselves that the risks are real.❜❜

WHY DO PEOPLE SMOKE?

"After the first few drags, I could feel a kind of warmth coming over me."

Smoking is a strange thing to do, isn't it? Especially when you think that not much happens. Tobacco doesn't make you drunk, like alcohol. Smokers don't get really high, like they do with marijuana. Why do so many people smoke cigarette after cigarette, day after day, year after year? Many are like slaves to the habit, with little idea why they do it.

When questioned more closely, however, people do begin to think about why they smoke. They often discover

The ritual of offering cigarettes can strengthen group identity.

that it is for some minor, unimportant reason that certainly isn't worth all the health risks involved.

I smoke because . . .

For a few people, tobacco can have a pleasant taste and smell (although most of us do not like to sit near a person who smells like an old ashtray). Others find it reassuring to have a cigarette in their mouths, like a baby sucks his thumb or uses a pacifier.

Having something to do with your hands also helps some people. It gives them confidence and a distraction at times when they might be nervous. Look at people before exams or job interviews, on trains and in airports. See how often they play with lighters, packs of cigarettes and ashtrays. Having cigarettes to share is one way of making friends, and staying part of a group.

❝❝ *Neil was the first, probably 'cause he was the oldest, and anyway his brother was already on 10 a day. We all sort of followed on.* ❞❞

These reasons go some way to explaining why people start to smoke. Smoking cigarettes also makes people look "good," or "cool," or "adult." But the smart and sophisticated image of smoking is fading fast. It now seems that smokers are harming themselves and the people around them.

But none of these explanations is the real answer to why people, once they have started, keep smoking. Most people continue to smoke tobacco because of the drug it contains – nicotine.

Tired or anxious? Have a cigarette . . .

Aside from the "pleasure" of cigarettes, some smokers talk about the "usefulness" of tobacco.

Some people say they smoke mostly to keep themselves alert and awake, and to help them concentrate. So cigarettes seem to act as a stimulant. Other people say they use cigarettes to calm themselves down, to make them relax and feel less twitchy. So for them, cigarettes are acting like a tranquilizer or a depressant.

It seems strange that nicotine can do both things. The answer seems to lie in the amount of drug taken. A little nicotine can make you feel more alert, and a lot can make you feel calm. The details are still unclear, but that's the broad picture.

Tobacco is taken in several ways, although smoking is the most common.

chewing a wad

sniffing snuff

smoking a cigarette

Inhaling: the seven-second nicotine fix

Tobacco can be used in other ways besides smoking. It can be chewed as a wad or "quid," or it can be chopped into a fine dust and sniffed into the nose, as snuff. These ways have one thing in common. They are very good at getting nicotine into the body.

Chewing tobacco allows nicotine to pass through the thin, moist lining of the mouth into the blood vessels underneath. Nicotine also gets into the blood when pipe and cigar tobacco is held in the mouth. Much the same happens when snuff is sniffed into the nose, with the nicotine passing through the thin lining of the nose into the blood vessels beneath.

But taking smoke into the lungs is the most effective way of dosing the body with the nicotine drug. The lining of the lungs is very thin and has millions of bubble-shaped pockets in it. Flattened out, this lining has an area the size of a tennis court. And the lungs have a large blood supply. The drug passes from the smoke in the lungs, across the thin lining, into the blood, and then along the bloodstream to the brain, in less than seven seconds! It is almost as effective as the drug addict's "mainline" injection.

At first, inhaling (breathing the cigarette smoke deeply down into the lungs) is unpleasant. The body reacts against it, as many people find out when they first try a cigarette. They cough and choke and feel sick. Inhaling makes sense only as a way of getting a drug to the brain.

> **Sometimes I was really gasping for a cigarette. After the first few drags, I could feel a kind of warmth coming over me. Partly it was the stuff in the smoke, I suppose. But part of it was having a cig on the go, a sort of companion.** "

You can pass cigarettes around a group, and look cool with one hanging out of your mouth, and use one to disguise that you are nervous – all without inhaling the smoke. The fact that people almost always inhale shows that cigarette smoking is really a kind of drug use.

Why choose tobacco?

Most plant leaves can be smoked. Many would smell and taste just as good as tobacco. But they are nearly all ignored. The choice of tobacco is probably not an accident. It can be explained by the nicotine the leaves contain. Other plant substances that are smoked, such as opium and marijuana, also have drugs in them which alter the way the body works.

We know that smokers take nicotine into their bodies, because we can measure it in blood and urine.

What does nicotine do?

Experimental studies show when rats are placed in cages and exposed to tobacco, they will press a lever to get

Cigarette ad, before smoking's health risks were fully known.

13

nicotine in their drinking water. Monkeys can learn to give themselves small doses of the drug. It appears that animals find nicotine addictive.

We do not know for sure why this is, but it is likely that nicotine affects parts of the brain called "pleasure centres." These are extremely small areas which are active when we have pleasant sensations, from eating to sex. In experiments, animals will do tricks and "work" to have these bits of their brains stimulated with a weak current of electricity.

Smokers seem to give themselves pleasure by taking nicotine, which passes from the blood to the brain's "pleasure centers." But the feeling of "pleasure" from nicotine is very short-lived.

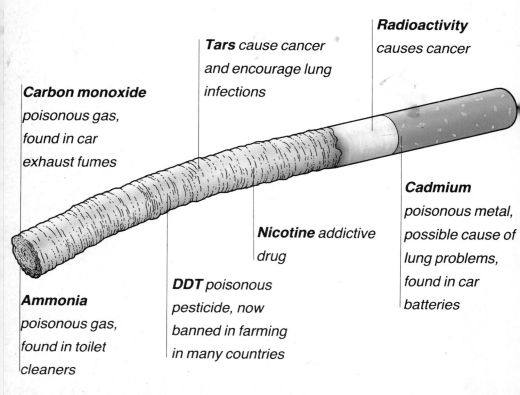

Radioactivity causes cancer

Tars cause cancer and encourage lung infections

Carbon monoxide poisonous gas, found in car exhaust fumes

Cadmium poisonous metal, possible cause of lung problems, found in car batteries

Nicotine addictive drug

Ammonia poisonous gas, found in toilet cleaners

DDT poisonous pesticide, now banned in farming in many countries

STARTING TO SMOKE

"The first cigarette was horrible. It almost made me throw up."

In many places, lots of people try their first cigarettes when they are about 12 years old. It varies a lot depending on the neighborhood and the person's background, but having a first cigarette at that age is typical. Often the cigarettes have been begged, borrowed or taken from someone older, perhaps a big brother or sister or an older friend or even a parent.

Why should people want to try a cigarette when they almost certainly know that it's bad for them, that it can cost a lot of money, and that they could end up as heavy smokers and die because of it?

Reasons for starting to smoke

Natural curiosity is one reason. Another is being "in" with friends. Smoking is usually first tried as one of a crowd.

Smoking is not actually illegal. So it's not the same kind of protest against authority as stealing is, or trying a harder and illegal drug like heroin. But smoking when an adolescent is usually frowned on. It is something we are told not to do. So doing it is a way of establishing a kind of independence. The idea is that it's something set apart for adults: by doing it yourself, you'll seem adult.

In fact, the opposite is true. Many people think that two out of three adults smoke, when it is really one in three. And when you realize that most smokers wish they'd never started, things become very different.

Starting young: children often smoke to copy the adults around them

Family and friends

Having others around who smoke makes it more likely that a person will take up the habit. That goes for mothers, fathers, older brothers and sisters, and for teachers, priests, youth leaders and similar people. Anyone who is respected may be imitated too. Many rock stars, film stars and successful sportsmen and women are very aware that younger people look up to them and may copy them. Often, if they do smoke, they do it away from the cameras.

But the most important influence seems to be friends, especially older ones. Having a part-time job, more money and concentrating on out-of-school activities also encourages smoking.

Learning to smoke

Taking smoke into the lungs isn't a natural thing to do. At first your body fights against it. You have to learn to inhale – to breathe in the smoke, deep into your lungs. Learning is often unpleasant. People usually cough and choke the first few times. This is the body's natural and sensible reaction against poisonous and irritating substances pouring into its fragile, delicate lungs. But after some practice, most people unfortunately learn to overcome these reactions.

The first cigarette was horrible. It almost made me throw up. But I didn't want to a failure in front of my mates, so I kept on at it. After a few, it got a bit better.

So the first few cigarettes are often unpleasant. The smoke may make you choke, feel dizzy and light-headed, or even be sick. This is enough to discourage many people. But others persist. Once the body gets a little used to nicotine, the unpleasant effects wear off.

Stopping and starting again

When they are young, many people smoke a few cigarettes, stop, and then take up smoking again. At this stage, we are very easily influenced one way or the other. Smoking may not seem too serious a problem. After all, if you can quit once, you can quit again. It's obvious that the first few cigarettes don't make you an addict. But regular smoking can quickly become a strong habit.

Stress is often given as a reason for starting again.

People in high-pressure jobs often say they smoke to ease the stress.

People who have given up for years will crave a cigarette when they've had a fight, or someone dies, or they lose a job, or a boyfriend or girlfriend leaves. They think that one or two cigarettes will help them get by when things are difficult. But first it's one, then another, then suddenly a whole pack.

Starting to smoke because of stress may be a particularly bad idea. If you can take a step or two back, problems may not seem so great. Talk to someone about them, rather than lighting up a cigarette and worrying on your own. In the long run, starting to smoke is really just adding another problem.

Taking an occasional cigarette from friends is just as risky. Sooner or later you feel you have to pay them back.

❝ Convention denies high school students the right to enjoy the 'pleasures' of tobacco, gambling and alcohol. Their mystery makes them seem of special value ❞

BECOMING A REGULAR SMOKER

"I found if I lit a cigarette it got me over the next five minutes."

Smoking for pleasure, and using nicotine as a kind of tool to alter the way you feel, could make smoking seem worthwhile. But these "benefits" are tiny compared with the health costs of smoking. After a while, any advantages that there may be in smoking no longer apply. As the body comes to depend on nicotine more and more, the effects of nicotine become less and less.

Starting with good intentions

People may begin with the idea that they'll only smoke a few cigarettes. The idea is that smoking will heighten the pleasure of being with friends. Or perhaps it is to relax, or to feel less rushed or less nervous. But drugs, including nicotine, don't work like that.

It can be so easy for people to have more and more cigarettes, and they will smoke at every opportunity. Even though the cigarettes no longer have the same effect, he or she can always find a reason to smoke them. Soon the person is lighting a new cigarette up every half an hour, and every day sees another empty pack.

Suddenly instead of using cigarettes you are letting them use you. You used to have a cigarette to make you feel specially good, now you have one to avoid feeling bad. How does this change happen?

❝❝ *If I lit up, I found that I could get over the next ten or fifteen minutes. I began to use smoking as a way of coping.* **❞❞**

Getting hooked

Our bodies like to be in balance. When something comes along that produces a change in one direction, the body pushes back, to return to where it was. The body does not like having its chemistry interfered with.

So when a chemical comes along and produces a change, the body compensates. This means that when the chemical disappears, the body is out of balance once more, but in the opposite direction.

For example, a stimulant drug increases our alertness. The body responds by pushing in more of its own natural substances, which have a dampening and depressing effect. Gradually the two balance each other out, and we are back where we started. Then if the stimulant drug is taken away the body overbalances into depression. It is still making its depressant chemicals, but the drug the chemicals were acting against is no longer there.

This rebound effect is the basis of addiction. It explains what happens when we become dependent on a drug, and then suddenly it is not there. The state is called withdrawal.

❝ Once I was actually shaking. I did the old trick of spilling my matches trying to light up. ❞

What happens with nicotine is similar. The body gets used to the drug. Take it away, and we feel bad. If the drug is kept away the body regains its normal, healthy balance. But that takes time, and it is often easier just to give in and restore the balance by smoking another cigarette.

Addiction is a vicious circle

Many people smoke regularly because they are trying to maintain nicotine levels in the body. Nicotine travels quickly from the lungs to the brain, but it also starts to disappear just as quickly from the body. Within about half an hour of finishing a cigarette, half the nicotine taken in has gone.

As the nicotine level drops, the smoker begins to feel worse. He or she may be depressed or irritable. So he or she lights another cigarette and feels good again. But that response just makes things worse. The body becomes more used to nicotine, and the person becomes more used to the idea that the only way to deal with feeling bad is to smoke.

This is the vicious circle of addiction. Not everyone gets into it, but most smokers do. It's what makes giving up so difficult – even when they know there are the best reasons in the world for quitting.

❝❝ *The first time I was offered cigarettes was by this boy, a year older than me. I liked him. I didn't want to look stupid in front of him, so I took one. When I started to cough, he laughed. he knew it was my first cigarette.* **❞❞**

Not so new

It's not just recently that we have come to realize smoking is addictive. When Christopher Columbus became the first European to discover America, in 1492, he saw the Indians "drinking smoke." The smoke came from burning the leaves

Most people don't smoke. Two out of three are non-smokers.

of a strange New World plant, tobacco, and the Indians weren't drinking it, but inhaling it.

Soon this plant was brought to Europe, where it grew well in the warmer parts, and smoking gradually spread all over the world. Even in those days, however, wise people saw the addictive nature of smoking, although they didn't know it was caused by nicotine. King James I of England tried to persuade smokers to stop. Murad the Cruel of Turkey cut off their heads. But they wouldn't stop then, and some still won't today.

Cigars were developed about a hundred and fifty years ago. Even at that time their health risks were suspected, and one wit described them as "a fire at one end and a fool at the other."

Cigarettes as we know them today started about a hundred years ago. But cigarette smoking did not become really popular until World War I, when soldiers spread the habit. The filter tip appeared before World War II. At first the filter was intended to save money by using up space in the cigarette that would otherwise have to be filled by expensive tobacco.

Gradually cigarettes became more and more popular. Until some thirty years ago the majority of people in the Western World smoked them. Now the times are changing.

WHAT SMOKERS DIE OF

"What really frightened me was when I coughed up blood."

In the 1950s, more and more people were dying from lung cancer. Doctors started to ask these cancer patients about their lives. Smoking was one of the topics many of them had in common. They quickly found that many with lung cancer smoked cigarettes. It was also clear that those dying of cancer tended to be those who smoked most. Nine out of every ten cases of lung cancer were found in people who smoke cigarettes.

The smoker's cough

Smoking damages the linings of the air tubes in the lungs. The linings are less able to do their normal job of keeping the lungs clean. Normally they filter out dust and other particles and bring them up into the throat, where they can be coughed up and swallowed. Smoking stops them doing this, so the particles collect and clog the airways.

In a smoker's lungs there is a second problem – a load of heavy, sticky tar that settles into the air tubes overnight. The result is that when smokers get up in the morning, they have to cough hard to try and get rid of this tar. Sometimes they cough so hard that blood vessels in the lungs break, and they cough up blood. This morning bout of coughing is a bad sign, and it could be an early warning of cancer.

When I was a little girl, I used to wake up early and listen to my parents coughing, til they retched. Every morning. It was the best anti-smoking ad you could ever have.

The risks of lung cancer

The pattern is simple. The more you smoke, the greater the risk of developing lung cancer. Smoke ten cigarettes a day, and you are ten times more likely than a non-smoker to get cancer. Smoke 20, and you run 20 times the risk. And so on.

Doctors soon learned that there was a definite connection between cancer and smoking. But the connection wasn't absolute proof that smoking caused cancer. It was vaguely possible that the kind of people likely to get cancer were also the kind of people likely to smoke – just by coincidence.

So the next step was to see what happened when some of the smokers gave up. The group of people that gave up first were doctors. (They didn't wait for absolute proof that smoking causes cancer. The initial studies were good enough for them.)

The results pretty much proved the case. As soon as the doctors gave up cigarettes, their chances of dying from lung cancer started to drop. When people had stopped for 10 to 15 years, their chances of getting lung cancer were the same as those of someone who had never smoked. People who continued smoking, however, died at the same rate.

❝ I began to lose weight. I started to cough more, and I was panting and wheezing. Then they said it was the Big C. I remember coming to in the hospital after the op and automatically thinking, 'God, I could do with a cigarette . . .' ❞

Saving human lives

Scientists in laboratories also played a part in showing that smoking causes cancer. As you know from looking at the stained end of a cigarette filter, tobacco smoke contains sticky brown tar. When this tar was painted onto the skin of a mouse, it caused cancer there. And chemists analyzing the tobacco tar showed that it contained substances known to produce cancer.

In the smoking laboratory, cigarette fumes are analyzed.

Some people did not believe this evidence. They said that the skin of a mouse is not the same as the lining of the lung. Also, tobacco tar on its own is not exactly the same as cigarette smoke. So scientists had to find out in the most direct way possible whether cigarette smoke caused lung cancer. So there were experiments in which dogs and other animals were made to breathe the smoke from cigarettes. The dogs had masks on and breathed only smoke. It was unpleasant but it gave even stronger evidence that smoking causes lung cancer. It has helped save many human lives.

How does lung cancer start?
It still isn't known exactly how lung cancer happens. Tar droplets are breathed in, and tend to land in the large tubes that take air into the lungs. This is the precise place where most lung cancer starts in humans. The tar irritates the sensitive lining of the air passages, while certain chemicals in it damage the microscopic cells that make up the lining. These cells are multiplying all the time and replace older ones that die.

For many years, the body is able to repair the damage caused by tar. And in some smokers (luckily), the cells never go out of control. But sooner or later in other smokers, the damage to the cells is not repaired. A single cell becomes cancerous and starts to multiply when it should not. From this single event, a growth, or tumor develops and spreads – not just in the lungs, but throughout the body.

If nobody smoked, nine out of 10 people who now die from lung cancer would not get this disease. But there would still be a few cases. This is because cancer-causing chemicals are also found in other forms of smoke, for example in polluted fumes from vehicles and factories, in industrial processes and even in garden bonfires. There are also chemicals like asbestos that cause lung cancer, as well as the possibility of radiation from nuclear disasters.

Other cancers caused by smoking

Lung cancer is the main form of cancer caused by smoking. But tobacco also causes other kinds of cancer. Smoking increases the risk of cancer of the mouth and throat, especially in someone who is a heavy drinker as well as smoker. Tobacco that is chewed or used as snuff almost certainly leads to cancer of the mouth and nose. So these ways of using tobacco are not safe.

The lungs of a smoker (left), tar-blackened, and a non-smoker (right).

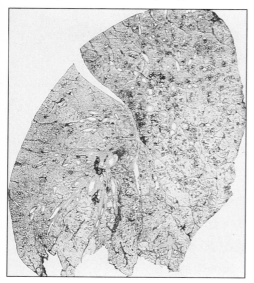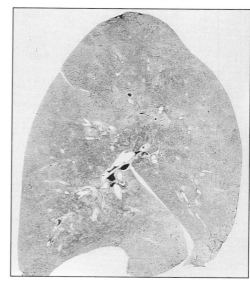

Smoking and heart disease

The disease most linked with smoking is lung cancer. But cancer is mostly a disease of older age. So you have to wait a long time before seeing whether cigarettes will give you lung cancer. But heart disease happens much younger. It is by far the biggest killer in middle age. This is because heart conditions in general are so common. In the United States five million people have heart disease. Half a million die from it each year, mostly from heart attacks. Cigarettes contribute to over a quarter of all deaths from heart disease.

> 🙶 *It was when my grandson had just started to walk and run, I had my first heart attack.* 🙷

The more cigarettes you smoke, the greater the risk of heart disease. The longer you smoke, the worse your chances are.

> 🙶 *My dad was always worried about smoking, and he always said to us never to start. He wasn't much of an example, we thought. A few years ago he had his first heart attack. It took that to shake him and stop him smoking.* 🙷

How does tobacco cause heart disease?

Heart attacks happen for two reasons. First, fats build up in the small arteries that supply the heart muscle with blood. This happens over many years. But gradually the blood vessels become more and more narrow. This process is faster if we eat fatty foods, if we do not exercise and if we smoke.

But the immediate cause of the heart attack is often the sudden blocking of a narrowed heart artery by a blood clot. This cuts off the supply of oxygen to heart muscle, which dies. Smoking also increases the chances of a blood clot.

The main health risks from smoking.

- *cancer of the mouth and throat*

- *smoker's cough*

- *heart disease*

- *lung cancer*

- *hardened and narrowed blood vessels*

- *bronchitis and other chest infections*

We know it's the tar in cigarette smoke that causes lung cancer. But we do not know exactly why smoking damages the heart. It could be nicotine, which makes the heart beat faster and increases blood pressure. Nicotine also makes the blood more likely to clot.

But the culprit might just as easily be carbon monoxide, one of the many poisonous gases in tobacco smoke. Carbon monoxide is the toxic gas from car exhaust and is fatal. In smokers, carbon monoxide cuts down the amount of oxygen the blood can carry around the body.

Whatever the reason, smoking increases the chances of an early death from heart disease.

Other aspects of our life are important too, of course. Taking care about what we eat, exercising regularly and staying slim all reduce the risk of heart disease. But the biggest help to the heart is not smoking.

Lung infections and breathing problems

In some smokers, cigarettes cause lung cancer. But every smoker's body is damaged to some extent. The lungs simply work less well, and with age, they get worse faster than in non smokers. A smoker aged 40 has the lungs of a non-smoker aged 70.

But you can tell the difference between a smoker and a non-smoker even at the age of 20. Smoking means you are out of breath more easily. You don't have to smoke many cigarettes to get a smoker's cough. Smoking also increases the chances that your lungs will become infected, causing bronchitis.

❞❞ *The lift was always breaking down. One day I walked up the stairs with the computer engineer. Halfway up, he looked at me. I realized I was wheezing and panting . . . he was fine.* **❞❞**

Smoking and the unborn child

Women who smoke have smaller babies. On the average, they are about half a pound lighter. This is partly because the carbon monoxide gas in cigarette smoke cuts down the amount of oxygen in the mother's blood and therefore the amount of oxygen available to the baby in the womb is less. Such babies are also more likely to die either before birth or just after.

As a pregnant woman smokes, nicotine passes from her blood into her unborn baby's. After birth this drug also passes into breast milk. The baby of a mother who smokes certainly has a poorer start in life.

Smoking bothers other people

If you smoke, you are harming not only yourself but others – often those who are dearest to you. Evidence is mounting that "passive" or "secondary" smoking (breathing other people's cigarette smoke) causes ill health. Children brought up in homes where people smoke have many more lung problems, such as bronchitis and pneumonia. If you are a parent and a smoker, do you really want to harm your children like this?

Smoking during pregnancy gives the baby a poorer start in life.

As more and more people give up smoking or never start, people in general get used to less smoke being around — especially in public places such as trains, planes, cinemas, libraries and so on. Many factories and offices are becoming no-smoking areas, for health reasons as well as the terrible fire hazard from matches and cigarettes.

Second-hand smoke irritates the eyes and throat. For people with problems like asthma, it can make life a misery. Nicotine, tar and carbon monoxide find their way to everyone in a roomful of smoke. In fact, there is more nicotine, tar and poison gas in the "sidestream" smoke that drifts from a cigarette, than there is in the "mainstream" smoke taken into the smoker's lungs. Almost certainly some non-smokers become ill because of it.

ONCE A SMOKER, ?

"Fingerprints are yellow-brown with nicotine and clouds of smoke eddy round the TV screen."

People may give reasons about why they smoke, such as nervousness, or stress, or wanting to be part of the crowd. But is there something more? Are some people "born to smoke?" Maybe there's something in the smoker's personality that makes him or her more likely to take risks, or use drugs, than other people. Does the pressure from advertisers, or sponsors, or society in general, almost "force" certain types of people to smoke?

Are smokers different?

Smokers as a group are slightly different from non-smokers. But we shouldn't overplay this fact. The differences appear only when you take large numbers of smokers and compare them with large numbers of non-smokers. They are differences that you find on average. They can't be applied to individual people, since smokers and non-smokers overlap to such an extent. And they certainly don't suggest that people are "stuck" in one group, or that smoking is in any way worthwhile.

So what are the differences? Smokers tend to drink more coffee than non-smokers. They also drink more alcohol, and they are more likely to have tried other mind-altering drugs such as marijuana and amphetamines. This may suggest that smokers are more interested in experimenting. It may mean that they are people who like to use drugs to control their moods.

Smokers also tend to change jobs more often and marry more often. They are more likely to get divorced, and they tend to have more traffic accidents. They are also less

Pipe or cigar smokers are also at risk, especially from mouth cancer.

likely to wear seat belts. So smokers seem to accept risks more easily, and they seem to have more of an appetite for change. These facts suggest an underlying difference in personality.

Personality

Smokers tend to be a little more extrovert than non-smokers. That is, they seek the company of others and are more outgoing. They may act emotionally rather than thinking first.

Now, you could say that these differences are there because of smoking. If you take up smoking, perhaps you'll start to go out more. And perhaps one of nicotine's effects on the brain is to make people more emotional. But we now know these differences are found before people start to smoke, not afterwards. So they are not the result of smoking itself, or nicotine. It seems that some of these differences are inherited from parents. Having a mother or father who smokes makes it more likely that a child will smoke, even if the child is brought up by someone else who is a non-smoker.

All these differences between smokers and non-smokers are real, but they are quite small. What happens in the environment – at school and in the family home – is probably more important. The more smokers a person sees, the more likely he or she is to smoke. Especially if these people are looked up to and respected as role-models.

The worldwide drive against smoking: a sign in Moscow's Red Square.

Place in society

Many millions of people have stopped smoking over the past 20 years. Most of them have been well educated, with more money and better jobs. This means that most smokers nowadays come from groups that are least well-off, such as those with semi-skilled or unskilled jobs, or with no jobs at all.

This has widened the gap between smokers and non-smokers. In the United States college graduates are only half as likely to smoke as those who dropped out of school as soon as they could. The same is true in Britain. Two people out of five people in unskilled jobs smoke, compared to only one in five professional people.

> *In the poorer houses, just about everybody smokes. Ashtrays are full of butts. Fingertips are yellow-brown with nicotine and clouds of smoke eddy round the TV screen.*

Smoking and society

To smoke or not to smoke: this is a decision that must be left up to the individual. But we all live together in society, and each of us is affected by what other people do. The efforts of those who make, sell and advertise cigarettes, as well as what the government says, all have an effect.

Except for banning the sale of tobacco to children under age, smoking is legal. But that doesn't mean society has no interest in it. The costs of ill health, diseases and

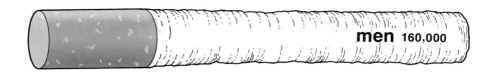

Annual deaths from smoking-related diseases.

deaths caused by smoking are enormous. There are millions of days lost from work because of illnesses due to smoking, which makes companies less efficient. There are hospital bills to pay for people with lung cancer and heart disease. There are pensions to pay when the breadwinner dies, and the spouse and children are left on their own.

Smoking also does enormous damage by starting fires. The soccer stadium fire at Bradford, England in 1986 burned 50 people to death. It was started by a cigarette butt.

Taxes

Some of the costs of illness and care needed by smokers are met by taxes which the government gets from tobacco sales. There is a myth that these taxes help the economy, and that smokers "pay their way." This is not true. Far more money is spent on dealing with the problems caused by smoking.

Governments have great influence on what people do simply by raising prices. As the cost of a pack of cigarettes increases, fewer are sold. Most of the price of a pack of cigarettes is already tax.

But the changes must be gradual, for two reasons. First, people who really cannot give up cigarettes should not be unfairly treated.

Second, tobacco companies and the people who work in them need time to change. If they are warned, the companies can move into other kinds of business. They can make their profits and provide jobs without killing people. The farmers who grow tobacco also need time to find other crops. But this cannot happen overnight. It needs time.

Compulsory warnings on cigarette packs are changed regularly.

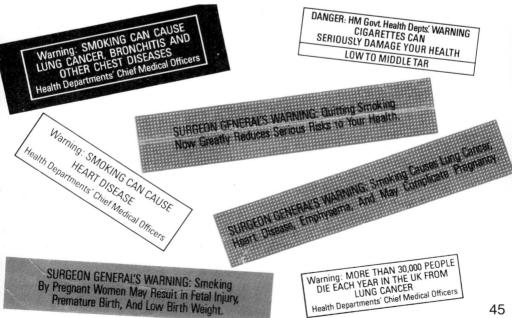

Warning: SMOKING CAN CAUSE LUNG CANCER, BRONCHITIS AND OTHER CHEST DISEASES
Health Departments' Chief Medical Officers

DANGER: HM Govt. Health Depts.' WARNING
CIGARETTES CAN SERIOUSLY DAMAGE YOUR HEALTH
LOW TO MIDDLE TAR

SURGEON GENERAL'S WARNING: Quitting Smoking Now Greatly Reduces Serious Risks to Your Health.

Warning: SMOKING CAN CAUSE HEART DISEASE
Health Departments' Chief Medical Officers

SURGEON GENERAL'S WARNING: Smoking Causes Lung Cancer, Heart Disease, Emphysema, And May Complicate Pregnancy.

SURGEON GENERAL'S WARNING: Smoking By Pregnant Women May Result in Fetal Injury, Premature Birth, And Low Birth Weight.

Warning: MORE THAN 30,000 PEOPLE DIE EACH YEAR IN THE UK FROM LUNG CANCER
Health Departments' Chief Medical Officers

45

Advertising and education

All over the world, governments warn of the dangers of smoking. The message is clear from departments of health and the Surgeon General of the United States. Governments even warn us on cigarette packs that smoking is bad for us.

But while governments spend millions, tobacco companies spend billions – on advertising, sponsorship of sporting events and public relations.

In many places, advertising is controlled. Companies can't suggest that smoking brings wealth and success with the opposite sex, for example. They are mostly not allowed to appeal to young people, and they are not supposed to claim that smoking is healthy.

But tobacco companies have been clever at bypassing many of these rules. Cigarette ads certainly are seen by young people. They are often placed deliberately where they will be. And the association between smoking and health is still allowed through the sponsorship of sports events. It also comes across in the pictures used, such as linking cigarettes with a romantic evening or the great outdoors.

So governments could do much more to bring a balance between education and advertising. This is the least that's needed. Most doctors think all advertising and promotion of cigarettes should be banned, completely and forever.

Cigarette ads are restricted in the image they might convey.

Women

About 50 years ago, it became more accepted for women to smoke. (Before then it had been a men-only habit.) Many women started, smoking mainly cigarettes.

About 30 years ago, deaths from lung cancer started to rise in women. They are still rising. Heart disease too is increasing in women. And for women who take the "pill" (oral contraceptive), smoking multiplies any risks.

Tobacco companies know this. But they are still trying to sell more cigarettes to women. They do it by launching special brands, and by adverts suggesting cigarettes make women equal to men in a generally male world. But this will be equality in death as well as life.

HOW TO
STOP

"I worked it out . . . at 20 a day, that's a couple of albums a week . . ."

Stopping early is easier than stopping late. If you've smoked for only a few months or years, you are unlikely to have much of a problem. The longer you have smoked, the more difficult quitting becomes. Even so, it is never too late. Within a few weeks of stopping your lungs will begin to clear and your senses of smell and taste will sharpen. Within a year or two you'll be less breathless. About 10 to 15 years after stopping, your chances of developing lung cancer will be about the same as those of a non-smoker.

Making the decision

Stopping for good needs a firm decision. You may be helped by the fact that you probably don't see yourself as a real smoker, fading into old age (if you make it that far) in a haze of tobacco fumes and coughing. You're more likely someone who is trying it out, just to say you did it.

The quickest and best way to stop smoking is to stop now, quickly and completely. In the long run, the more tricks and excuses and "aids" you need to help your own willpower, the more likely you are to start again.

Coping at first

If stress was one of your reasons for smoking, find other ways of dealing with it. Talk through problems with another person. Try breathing slowly and regularly, to get back in control of your body. Each time you want to light up, make yourself wait for five minutes. You'll be surprised at how the longing will pass.

The feeling of "needing" another cigarette is due to

falling nicotine levels in your body. Make up your mind that it's you who's in control, not some strange chemical.

People and places

When it comes to being with other people who smoke, practice saying "No." Make it friendly but firm. Make sure they know you are giving up, and ask them not to offer you any more cigarettes. Family members and good friends will respect these wishes. In fact they may well be envious and join with you in stopping. Giving up smoking in a group with collective willpower and helping each other is often very successful.

 All four of us stopped together. Tracy gave in after about 10 minutes, but we all stuck it. **"**

Smoking and the Third World

Many tobacco companies have made up for the drop in cigarette sales at home by increasing exports to Africa, Asia and South America. Many cigarettes sold there are high tar and nicotine brands banned in our countries.

They have also been using ads suggesting that smoking brings style, sex and success. These ads are not allowed in Europe and North America. In addition, farmers in the Third World are encouraged to grow tobacco instead of food crops, so they depend on the money made from tobacco.

But this unfairness won't be allowed to continue. The World Health Organization of the United Nations is exposing

EXCUSES, EXCUSES

"I'm afraid of getting fat if I stop"
Smokers weigh slightly less than non-smokers, on average.
And some people who stop smoking put on weight. But the
amounts are small. A little less sugar or a little more
exercise will more than restore the balance.

"There's no proof that smoking causes lung cancer"
People who support the tobacco industry try to confuse us
by talking of "possible" health risks, or the smoking
"controversy". But there is nothing "possible" or
"controversial" about it. We can be as sure that smoking
causes cancer as we are that sewage bacteria in water
cause diarrhoea. No respected group of scientists believes
that smoking is harmless. The evidence is too strong and it
comes from too many different sources.

"It won't happen to me"
Well, it may not. You may be one of the lucky ones. We all
know regular smokers who have lived to old age. Not all
smokers get lung cancer or heart disease. But many of them
do. Three or four smokers in every 10 will die because of
their smoking.

"We all have to die of something"
True. Non-smokers don't live for ever. But not smoking is
certainly going to cut the chance of dying early. And it is
going to improve the quality of your life. Lungs and heart
stay healthier longer, and you'll be able to lead a more
active life.

the international tobacco trade. Governments throughout the world are becoming wise to the dangers of tobacco.

Banning smoking?

One idea that won't work is banning smoking itself. It's been tried through history and always failed. As soon as a ban arrives, so does a black market. It would be like the Prohibition era of the 1920s, when banning alcohol simply led to crime and corruption on a vast scale.

There is also another point. People should be given information about what is good for their health and then encouraged to stay healthy. But they can't be forced. If some people want to carry on smoking, that is their free choice, as long as they don't interfere with the rights of others.

Make a point of being in places where you shouldn't smoke. Choose the no-smoking areas in buses, trains, clubs, discos, restaurants, cinemas, and so on. At work, do something else when you'd normally light up. Switch to a new daily newspaper, read a new book, or do some exercise.

At home, throw away the ashtrays, the cigarettes, the lighters. Have nothing to do with them any more.

Looking forward

Most of what you gain from not smoking is long-term. A healthy heart and clean lungs in old age may be difficult to appreciate when you're young. Yet there are also immediate benefits. When you feel like a cigarette, think about

The way to stop: trash the ash and never look back.

these instead. You'll save money for clothes, records, concerts, food . . . whatever you like. You'll have the feeling of being in charge, in control.

> ❝ *I worked it out . . . 20 a day, that's a couple of albums a week . . . suddenly I had all this extra money.* ❞

There are lot of people out there who will try to get you started on cigarettes again, not least the tobacco manufacturers and advertisers. They had you hooked, but now, with your strength of will, you can swim freely. Soon you'll feel fitter, fresher, with more stamina.

Cutting down, then stopping

Gradually smoking fewer cigarettes works for some people, as a way of preparing to give up completely. But it is not a good idea for others. Once they get down to a certain level, they really start to want the next cigarette. Each puff becomes more rewarding and thus even more difficult to give up. The other reason is that the number of times they smoke may simply creep back up again.

Switching to a milder brand

Smoking a lower tar or "lighter" cigarette is not a good answer either. Many people who do this tend to smoke more cigarettes. They take more puffs, they take in more smoke with each puff and they inhale the smoke more deeply. All this may be an attempt to compensate for the weaker "taste," but it is more likely to be a way of increasing the amount of nicotine obtained from the cigarettes.

If you work hard to get more nicotine, you'll get more tar too, and more carbon monoxide. In terms of your health you may well be back where you started. So choosing a brand that is low on the tar charts, or which has low values of tar and nicotine written on the pack, probably makes little difference. At best, you might reduce your chances of getting a smoker's disease by about one quarter.

Doctors suspect that one reason mild cigarettes have been introduced is to make it easier for people to start smoking. The cigarette tastes mild mostly because there are tiny holes around the filter that let in air when you suck. The smoke is diluted and is easier to inhale. You won't feel so dizzy or sick as you will if you first try with a stronger cigarette. Many "light" brands have an image that appeals to the young, especially teenage girls. But in many ways they are just an easier road to addiction and illness.

What about pipes and cigars?

Provided you don't inhale the fumes, the risks of smoking a pipe or cigar are less than the risks of smoking cigarettes. There is less chance of heart disease and lung problems. But pipe and cigar smokers still suffer from cancers of the mouth and throat.

However, switching from cigarettes to a pipe or cigar is not as good as giving up smoking completely. Most people who try this tend to carry on inhaling.

 Once I got used to cigars, I went back to inhaling out of habit, and it was much worse!

Pills, potions and gums

Various gums, pills and potions claim they are the easy way to stop smoking. They are mostly useful as an aid to willpower and perhaps as a way of keeping your mouth occupied with something that isn't a cigarette. They don't do anything chemically to replace nicotine.

The exception to this is nicotine chewing gum, which is available in some countries from family doctors. This is very effective for addicted smokers who have been smoking heavily for many years. It is not likely to be much use to someone who is young.

Nicotine gum, which is chewed like ordinary chewing gum, allows nicotine to be taken into the blood through the thin lining of the mouth. It's really just a modern version of chewing tobacco. Smokers who truly can't do without nicotine in their lives can get enough from the gum. But they don't have the pleasure of smoking, since they don't get fast "shots" of nicotine to the brain, as they do when they inhale tobacco smoke. The idea behind the gum is that the unpleasantness of nicotine withdrawal is taken away, while the user comes round to the idea of breaking the habit itself.

Clinics and plans

Anti-smoking clinics and "5-day plans" also offer help. For some people, giving up in a support group setting is easier than giving up alone. Also, many smokers want someone to push them into a new routine while they quit.

Acupuncture has helped some people to quit smoking.

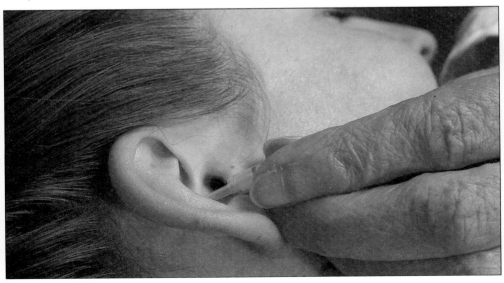

FACTFILE

What tobacco looks like

Tobacco is made from leaves of the tobacco plants, scientific names *Nicotiana tabacum* (in the West) and *Nicotiana rustica* (in some Eastern tobaccos). The plant is tall and leafy-looking, and it grows in most warm and temperate parts of the world where there are at least 120 frost-free days each year.

Growers have bred tobacco plants to yield many different sizes and shapes of tobacco leaf, suitable for different uses such as cigarettes, cigars and pipes.

The tobacco-harvester at work.

Harvesting and processing

Ripe leaves are picked by hand, though in some regions mechanical pickers have been developed. The leaves are dried or "cured" by various methods.

Flue curing in a specially heated and ventilated building is usually used for cigarette tobacco. Air curing, in the open but protected from direct sun and rain, is used for cigar tobaccos and some cigarette tobaccos. Fire curing is carried out over open fires in a smoky atmosphere, mainly for pipe tobaccos. Sun curing involves drying the leaves in the sunshine, for aromatic cigarette tobaccos.

Tell-tale signs of smoking

If you suspect someone of secretly smoking, there are several tell-tale signs which include:
- the smell of tobacco or stale ashes on their breath, clothing and hair (this can be difficult to detect by a person who smokes himself, or in a house where smokers live)
- boxes of matches or lighters hidden away, spent matches, cigarette ends, burn marks from stubbing out cigarettes, flakes of tobacco
- packs or empty wrappers for roll-your-own tobacco or papers which are often tried by young people with less money
- secretive behaviour

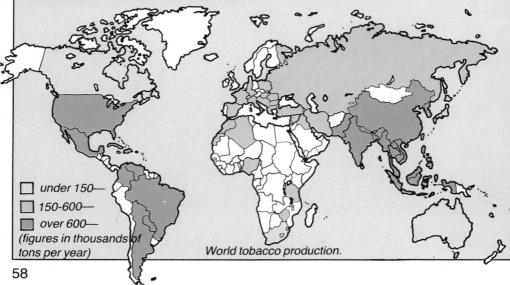

under 150—
150-600—
over 600—
(figures in thousands of tons per year)

World tobacco production.

TOBACCO PROFILE

Common name	Tobacco
Other names	Baccy, chew, wad, smoke
Name of drug involved	Nicotine
Drug type	Stimulant, possibly also a sedative
Made from	Leaves of the tobacco plant, dried (cured) and in the case of cigarettes shredded and mixed with various additives
Ways of taking	Mostly by smoking as cigarettes, but also smoked as pipe or cigar tobacco; also chewed as a wad, sniffed into the nose as snuff, or smeared around the inside of the mouth as a paste
Main effects	Can increase alertness and perhaps reduce anxiety
Addictiveness	One of the most addictive substances known
Other ingredients	Tars of various sorts which vaporize or form as droplets in the smoke; carbon monoxide, a poisonous gas; dozens of other substances
Risks	Cancer of the lungs, mouth and throat; other lung damage leading to increased likelihood of infections such as bronchitis and pneumonia; increased risk of heart disease
Main producer countries	Grown in many countries; China, United States, India, Brazil, South Africa and Turkey are among the leading growers
Main consumer countries	Large numbers of consumers in almost every country; nearly 50 million smokers in the United States
Example of cost	$1.50 for a packet of 20 cigarettes (although cost varies from store to store depending on local taxes)
Legal status	It is legal for anyone of any age to use tobacco in most countries;
Smoking statistics	National Institute of Drug Abuse (NIDA) conducts yearly surveys of high school seniors. Statistics for 1985 (Class of '86): 67% answered yes to the question, "Have you ever tried cigarettes?" 29.6% said they had had a cigarette in the last thirty days. Males: 27.9% Females: 30.6% In the previous thirty days, 18.7% said they had smoked one or more cigarettes per day, on the average: Males: 16.9% Females: 11.4%

More importantly, 30% of the adult population smokes cigarettes (32% of all males and 28% of females). |

SOURCES OF HELP

Up-to-date information

Action on Smoking and Health
2013 H Street, NW
Washington DC 20006
(202) 659 4310
Write or call for educational brochures and pamphlets.

Tobacco-Free Young America Project
224 E Capitol Street
Washington DC 20003
(202) 546 1750
This clearinghouse provides information on the latest tobacco studies and on state and local smoking legislation.

Help in stopping smoking
The American Cancer Society, the American Heart Association, and the American Lung Association have information or programs for people who want to quit smoking. Local Divisions of these organizations are listed in your area telephone book.

Office on Smoking and Health
Park Bldg 1-10
5600 Fishers Lane
Rockville MD 20857
(301) 443 5287
Provides a fact book on smoking and pamphlets on how to quit.

General information on drugs
These organizations do not deal with smoking tobacco as such, but can give advice to someone who smokes or takes other drugs.

Helping Youth Decide
National Association of State Boards of
Education
PO Box 1176
Alexandria, Va 22313
(703) 684 4000
Write for their free booklet about making informed decisions concerning smoking, drugs and other issues. They also organize parent-student workshops.

National Institute on Drug Abuse
1 (800) 522-H-E-L-P
This hotline is staffed from 9.00am on weekdays and from 12 noon to 3.00am on weekends. Counselors can talk with you, refer you to a drug treatment program, or answer questions about drugs, rehabilitation, health or legal problems.

New York State Division of Substance
Abuse Services
1 (800) 522 5353
This toll-free number reaches counselors who can provide referrals for treatment or legal advice, or over-the-telephone crisis intervention.

WHAT THE WORDS MEAN

addict someone who needs to keep taking a drug in order to remain "normal" and stave off withdrawal effects on the body and/or mind. "Addiction" has a slightly different meaning to "dependence", in that it usually refers to someone who has been dependent on a drug for some time, and it is more tied up with his lifestyle and society's view of him. In some countries "addict" it is a legal term, meaning someone who's registered on an official list as being dependent on a drug

cancer a group of diseases which usually involve the formation of a growth (lump or tumor) which is malignant, sending out "seedlings" that spread around the body to set up growths elsewhere

carbon monoxide a poisonous gas found in tobacco smoke which lowers the amount of oxygen carried around the body by the blood

dependence the need to keep taking a drug regularly, either for its effects on the body (to keep away withdrawal symptoms, for instance) or its effects on the mind (such as to make the user think he is "getting through the day")

drug any chemical or other substance that changes the body's workings (including the way the person's mind works, his behavior, etc.)

drug abuse non-medical drug use with harmful effects, on the abuser and possibly on others

drug misuse using drugs in a way which people in general would see as not sensible, or not acceptable, and possibly harmful

nicotine a stimulant drug found in tobacco and tobacco smoke, which has various effects on the body such as raising blood pressure, making the heart beat faster and in an irregular fashion, and reducing the appetite

tar when talking about tobacco, various dark, sticky substances floating as droplets in tobacco smoke, that collect in a smoker's lungs and increase the risks of lung cancer, bronchitis and other illnesses

tolerance when the body becomes used to a drug, so that the same dose begins to have less effect, and increasing doses must be taken for the same effect

withdrawal the effects on the body and mind when a person suddenly stops taking a drug after being dependent on it. The effects are usually unpleasant and with nicotine may include heart flutters, headaches, nervousness and edgy behavior, and depression

INDEX

Photographic Credits:
Cover and pages 4, 8, 21, 27, 34, 49 and 54: Vanessa Bailey; page 7: Spectrum; page 11: Action on Smoking and Health (ASH); pages 15 and 30: Zefa; pages 17, 19, 25 and 36: Network; pages 32 (both) and 57: Science Photo Library; page 34: Art Directors; pages 41, 42 and 46: Rex Features; page 58: Photosource.

DATE DUE

NOV 9 '88			
SEP 3 0 1992			
MAY 1 '93			
MAY 2 '93			
MAR 10 '94			
APR 0 3 1995			
APR 0 4 1995			
GAYLORD			PRINTED IN U.S.A.